Brenda Eldridge

Stepping into the Blue

Acknowledgements

'Humility' and 'Wherever I Am' appeared in *Big Blue Marble*,
Pocket Poets 53
'Contrasts' and 'Quiet Messenger' in *An Unexpected Harmony* (with
John Egan), Pocket Poets 72
'Horned Moon' in *Remnants and Reflections* (with John Egan),
Pocket Poets 145

Stepping into the Blue
ISBN 978 1 76109 460 6
Copyright © text Brenda Eldridge 2023
Cover image: Brenda Eldridge

First published 2023 by
GINNINDERRA PRESS
PO Box 3461 Port Adelaide 5015
www.ginninderrapress.com.au

Contents

Precariously Balanced

There are some who say
Our planet
Floats through space
On the back of a turtle

Beguiled by this notion
I made a model

Dabbed dark blue paint
On a small canvas
With my fingers
Creating a rough surface
Then added white
To my crested waves

A small seashell floats
On the vastness of my ocean
Perched on this
A white origami bird

Beneath the canvas
I glued cottonwool balls
To represent clouds

All this is balanced
On a black cast-iron
Turtle

I am that bird
Perched on a
Floating shell
Precariously balanced
Searching for
Knowledge
Meaning

How do we measure…

We measure an age of rock –
So many millions of years

How do we measure
An age of oceans

We learn of
Earth's surface plates
Their constant shifting
Causing earthquakes
Tsunami

Those dark depths –
Have they been here
As long as mountains

How do we measure time and water

Rivers run deep

Do they have names
Those rivers running deep
Within an ocean

If gravitational pull
Creates ocean tides
Does moon influence
Reach to depths
Where sunlight does not go

Deeper than thought
These mysteries…

Beneath the blue

Far deeper than light can reach
A watery sanctuary
No currents
All is still
Silent
Too dark to be named a colour

Obdurate
Rock formations
Towering

*

A mote of life
With tiny heartbeat
Drawn blindly
By a river of gentle pressure
Being swept along
And up

Fingers of light probe
Density thins
Blues emerge
Tiniest flicker of fin and tail
Darting
Blue becoming swirls of silver

Whales

No amount of pictures or film footage
Nor seeing a skeleton in a museum
Nor measuring the correct number of
Feet and inches across a large office
Prepared me for their sheer size

Being in the right place
At the right time
I watched them leap out of the water
As playful as dolphins
Leaving an arc of rainbow-filled spray
Witnessed the abandonment of crashing
Into the welcoming embrace of the sea

I watched in awe
Mother and baby
Lolling luxuriantly in a small bay
Softly calling to each other
Showing more tenderness
Than I had seen people do

From the hidden depths
Of vast oceans
They had come to this particular place
For birthing and nurturing
As their ancestors had done
For millennia
Following some imprinting
From when they could move
Unharmed around their world

Dolphins

A creature of this world
Of darkest blues paling
To turquoise and aqua

Silver-grey dolphin
Perfect sleek symmetry

A family working together
Feeding
Nurturing young

Racing
Diving
Leaping
Surfacing for breath
Smoothly cruising

As I struggled to stand
In great boiling waves
I looked directly
Into a calm gentle eye
Beak smiling
Gifting me
A sense of joyous wonder

Seals

All power and strength
Dark-skinned
Blending with the rocks they rest on

On land they lumber clumsily
Surprisingly fast
Fiercely protective
Urging youngsters into the blue
Teaching them to fish
Playfully swooshing
Making bubbles

While their eyes
Hold depths of knowledge
Beyond words –
Much like our newborn babies

Beaches

The beaches of my childhood
On the south coast of England
Were like layered cake
First smooth rounded rocks
Big enough to fit in the palm of my hand
But sun-warmed not too hard to walk on

Then came the sharp shale
Painful to bare feet
Becoming grit
Until at water's edge was sand
Reminding me of mud

I remember sunny days but
Only recall cold dull
Khaki-coloured waves rolling in
Gently perhaps but still
Sending me to seek shelter
Between my parents' deckchairs

Or else they roared in like wild creatures
To my child eyes
Higher than our front door at home
Something I feared
Would carry me away

*

Years later
On the other side of the world
I was welcomed by beaches
Of soft white sand
Dazzling and hot under a summer sun

Shells many shapes and colours
Some resting like butterflies
Others mother-of-pearl iridescence
And water –

Never had I imagined such blues
Such clarity

A Constant

Waves – a constant
No matter whether beneath
A clear blue sky
Or one blanketed by grey clouds
Heavy thunderheads
Or inky blue-black ones

At some point
Waves come to the end
Of their energy
They might roll and crash
Suck at sand and weed
Or barely turn over
More like a fringe of lace
Yet still they whisper

A constant…

Where does the cycle start?

We call bodies of water different names
For our convenience
When really it is all one ocean
There are no edges
No natural borders
Except where there is land

School tried to teach me
How salt water
Becomes cloud
Becomes rain
To fall on land
To fill rivers
To flow back to ocean…

Scientific exactitude
For the most part
Is wasted on me

It seems to be
Like the conundrum
'What came first
The chicken or the egg?'

It will happen
Whether I understand it
Or not

Horizon

I read yesterday that horizon is not there
I could grasp what the words meant
But it was like letting go of a safety net

Here I am looking out to sea
And there is no straight clear pencil line
Between sky and water
Only a smudge
Not because of my poor eyesight
But because they really don't meet

Of course I know that – logically
The same as I know Atlas
Isn't holding sky and earth apart
But he might be even if I can't see him
And what we call horizon
Might be a thinning of the veil
Between this world and another

Hovering Between

An invisible presence
Smudged the horizon
Allowing a distortion of the normal
No clear line between sea and sky
Who could tell
Where the white/grey became blue/grey
No billowing clouds
No aqua edged with pristine foam
No waves at all
No blue sky at all
Just a haze
A smudge
Where realities merged
Became one
And passage from one world to another
Not needing even a step or pace
A hovering between
So hard to come back from

Sea Fog

Dampness clings to my hair
To my clothes
Winter but not cold
In this dripping stillness

Waves persistently lap the shore
Nudging me to pay attention
Why I wonder
There is nothing to see
Not even the sea

Sky has come down in a grey pall
Sounds of ever-moving water
Cries of silver gulls
Are all muffled

There – rocking like a ship at anchor
A lone pelican
Black and white feathers
Almost lost in this greyness

I felt he was gently mocking me
And I laugh at myself
For wanting to strip off
And join him in the surging tide
Just to keep him company

Time-to-go-time

I wrote your name in the wet sand
Small waves slipped in silently
Embraced the letters
The sisters of the sea
Took you home

I didn't mean to keep you here so long
Or perhaps you needed to stay

We had the time together
We weren't allowed when you lived

There is comfort in having shared
This time that was ours
Nothing to do with anyone else…

But it was time-to-go-time –
Something Mother used to say
It is what I said to her in my prayers
A few days before she died

Not Religion

Time and time again
Drawn to a beach
To paddle along a waterline
Welcoming water
Cold or warm
Around my ankles
Aware of a longing
To go further in
To put my head
Below the surface
A baptism each spring
Not in a religious cult

Promise Fulfilled Again

A year ago
First swim of a new season
I lowered myself into a smooth sea
Feeling again being held
By invisible arms
Only satisfied when I had swum underwater
Then turning over without thought to float
To watch sun and moon together
Dizziness
Panic
Arms flailing wildly
Feet instinctively found the ocean floor

All through
Spring
Summer
Autumn
Winter
I plodded the waterline
Looking longingly at the blueness
Fear dogging my footsteps
Only allowing myself to go knee-deep

Spring came again
I donned bathers
Cycled to the beach
Swore at the bike pedal
That gouged a piece from my foot
As I put it down on the sand

I walked steadily into the water
Gasped a little at the chill
The sting of raw flesh
Pleased there was no seaweed
No prayer for courage
Just a deep breath
Pushed myself along and down
Completely submerged
In clear cold water
A few strokes to know I could still do it
Standing up
Laughing out loud like a child
For child I was again

I dared myself to float –
No dizziness!
I spread arms and legs
In total trust
Felt myself weightless
In an embrace like no other
I swam underwater briefly
Aware it was time-to-go-time

I pushed my bike along the beach
Feeling the suns warmth on my shoulders
Pondering how I had been doing this
For over thirty years
This same stretch of beach
Was it the same waves
That sounded like the hurrying footsteps
Of someone trying to catch up with me?

Walking unseen with them

To any onlooker I was always alone
Walking the waterline
As I have done in the early morning
Countless times over thirty years

I was not alone
I never am
Solitary perhaps
But never alone

In the whisper or crash of waves
Was   is   and ever shall be
The presence of my children
Running and playing
Keeping close
Voices and laughter
Ringing clear on the air

Watering Eyes

Cold sand almost dry
Bright in the sun
White foam gleaming
Wind ruffling my hair

My eyes squint
With a will of their own
Tears well and fall

Can I say it is the elements?
Does sorrow count
As an element
That makes me weep?

Mandala in the sand

I sat at the edge of the dunes
Sand soft   dry   clean
I was absorbing the news
That at last my children's father had died
No surprise

Tears stung my eyes
Through the rainbows I could see
My fingers absently drawing a pattern
Starting with a simple curve
That became like a seashell
An intricate design gradually appearing

Like the mandala I had drawn
He was a complex man
Who lives on in all of us

As if…

I rest my bicycle at the base
Of the sand dunes
I paddle in a roiling sea
Hi-vis jacket crackling snapping
In tugging winds
As if we could be as free as a kite
Soaring high
Perhaps never to land

As if…

Unseeing

Drawn into windswept sand
A perfect circle containing
A very complicated pattern
Beautifully symmetrical
Far beyond my artistic skills
Running haphazardly across the centre
The tyre marks of a bicycle

Who would do such a thing
Did they not see it
Why would anyone destroy this creation!

But then I often ask myself
That same question
When I look at what
We are doing to our planet home

Light and shadow

When strong southerly winds
Hissing with energy
Pour like a stream
Along a shell-strewn beach
Little humps of sand
Gather at each shell
As if huddling together for protection

Early morning brings a trick
Of light and shadow
That makes the shells
Seem much larger
And imagination does the rest…
Perhaps in Egypt beside mystical pyramids

Cliffs

Where cliffs rise from ocean depths
There is a monumental conflict
Of two opposing forces –
Water ever hungry to reclaim land
Unable to rest for a moment
Land eventually conceding defeat
Crumbling and falling in increments

We think we are safe
With earth beneath our feet
We stand on clifftops
Watch waves hurling themselves
In a thunder of white foam
That flies high
Delicate as lace
With the illusion of being
Lightweight as snowflakes
Till it lands with a punch
On the unwary

Only to find water infiltrates
One minuscule drop at a time
Eventually making the hardest rock
Unstable
Ready to capsize

Contrasts

The rocks withstand
the pounding of aeons
reluctantly relinquishing
each small fragment
to this unrelenting force

The ocean constantly changes colour
always white edges the waves
the wind sends spindrift flying
impossibly delicate
encrusted with diamonds

No one owns them

My roots are forever English
A child of nature – earthbound
A deep association with all growing things

As a young woman
I emigrated to Australia
Over fifty years later
I know I do not own this land
This is not my country

I am in awe of huge skies
Tumbling oceans
The wind

No one owns these
Yet they connect us all

Blowing cobwebs away

Thoughts gather like clouds
On a dreary day
Stillness doesn't heal
It becomes oppressive

Step outside and the slightest breeze
Whispering on my face
Flicking my hair
Sends cobwebs blowing away
And leaves me a gift
Of sand between the pages
Of my notebook

From the end of a jetty

Wind and sea are different
When I stand at the end of a jetty

A small distance from land
Sees sun sparkles race across
A choppy surface
Dancing like sprites
Among sheets of blazing silver
I can see not just feel
The wind pushing water along
Making it slosh and slurp
Around silvered wooden pylons

Spring

Spring in March or September
Is still the end of cheerless winter
Herald of warmth and new growth
A time of racing clouds
Sudden heavy showers
Gusty winds and hailstones

Energy

Lying in bed listening
To wind roaring through trees
It sounds much the same
As if I were standing on a beach
Listening to waves crashing to shore

I don't know how wind velocity is measured
Or when it becomes gale force something –
But if I fear the roof will blow off
Or when I struggle to place
One foot in front of the other –
I know the wind has a strength
I must respect

And if the waves
Make it difficult to keep my footing
Threatening to drag me out into their depths
I would be foolish indeed
To challenge all that energy
If I value my life

I think of wind and sea
As living beings
Setting their own terms of engagement

Not quite the same

I closed my eyes
Listening to waves rolling and crashing
I thought they sounded the same
As the wind last night
Except the song differed slightly –
The wind whistled as well

Too many questions

Does the wind run out of energy somewhere
Is it ever still
Is the air ever as still
As I imagine it to be sometimes

I know there are currents
Under the surface of the ocean
I learned there are rivers of rain
In the heavens

Murmurations of starlings
Soaring eagles
Are they swimming in the air

Unintended Arrogance

I accepted with little thought
A gift of a fancy telescope
Found it so difficult to see through
Uncomfortable because I became
A voyeur rather than worshipper
Of other beings in our night sky

What arrogance to intrude
Think I had the right
To give names
To shadows and shapes
They are so beautiful
Without my spying on them

Yet I marvel at photographs taken
By others with clever cameras
Or space probes
Delving deep into the blueness
I am in awe of our blue marble home
Floating round among the stars
But I need the wonder
The mystery of the unnamed

.

Wherever I am

I had heard so much
read so much
seen so many pictures
of stars above the desert
I hungered to experience them

I noted that the moon
while past the full
would be bright enough
to cast an extra magic glow
and they would appear
to be close enough
for me to reach up and touch them

But it seemed the gods
had other ideas
as cloud covered the sky
and all its hidden treasures

When we arrived home
I stood on our balcony
overlooking the tidal reach
and raised my eyes up
as I do every night
and the stars were there
like constant friends
visiting planets too
filling me with wonder
and a sense of belonging

Humility

We do not own the skies
we cannot even fly in them unaided
as birds and insects do
neither do we know
how far are the farthest reaches
of the universe

The oceans are not there
to do our bidding
no matter what the size or
clever design
our boats are at their mercy
even the land bows
to the mighty force of water

The winds blow where they will
we can borrow their power
for our use
but with the strength of a
cyclone or tornado
they can destroy everything
we try to build or grow

Will we learn humility
the way we learned
to be so arrogant
before it is too late?

Quiet Messenger

With the sun already dazzling
while still below the horizon
this morning the moon rose
in a sky almost bursting
with anticipation
of the new day

She will be there
for most of the day
patiently arcing across the heavens
a tiny flick of white
ever watchful
not eclipsed
only visible to those
who take the time
to look up
and stand and stare

Daylight Safety

I do wonder why
I feel I am safest
Under a clear blue sky

Sun-worshippers

In my heart I am no different
To the Ancient Ones
My spirit welcomes
The Sun each morning
Thankful it has appeared again
To give us the gift of life
For another day

I watch sunsets in awe
Dare to name the dread
Will it return
Or will we be cast adrift
Into the darkness

It's moments like these
That make me aware
Of how fragile everything is

Perfect Timing

With fascination I watch clouds
As they come racing in across the gulf
Stretching long fingers
Fan-like over the tidal reach
Especially in the evening
When a dying sun colours them
Brilliant pink and orange
No less spectacular
When they turn dark grey
Emphasising the pearlescence
Of late evening
Before darkness overtakes us all

Who Does That?

Who throws the grey blanket
Over us in the middle of the day
As if to tuck us up to bed?
Why do they want to shield us
From the blue of eternity?
Instead of feeling cosy
I feel stifled
Long to shrug off the oppression
Of heavy greyness
Yearn for that glimpse of blue sky
A shaft of sunlight
The signals that reassure me
All is well

Silver Lining

It is said every cloud has a silver lining
But I think they exaggerate a little

Yes it's true dark thunderheads
Can have a silver edge
Which accentuates their shape and density
But I see wisps of white
Drifting across the heavens
Nothing dramatic
More like bits of lost candy floss
Hoping a breeze will link them
To each other
Then they too will have gravitas
Swirling skirts trimmed with
Glorious silvery lace
Ready to go to the ball…

Nuances

I painted clouds on a canvas
And quickly learned
Almost imperceptible changes
From white to grey
Nestled among those billowing pillows
Nuances only seen when you really look
And laughingly try to recreate them

Unfettered

I read somewhere
We are able to see further at night
Because our vision isn't
Inhibited by things

I look into the night sky
See countless stars
Some brighter than others

I want to see
Golden staves and musical notes
Linking the stars
Like giant cobwebs
I long to hear this haunting music

Instead I hear the steady beating of my heart
Which keeps me grounded
While my mind and spirit fly unfettered

Not just a rumble

Night hid gathering clouds
It was the distant rumble of thunder
Which alerted me to an oncoming storm

Lightning flashed continuously
Dancing like a dervish
From one cloud to another
Filling the air with eerie light

Still the thunder rolled ominously

Then the world was split
By a fork of lightning
Brilliant silver blue
Linking heaven and earth
Gone so quickly
Yet leaving an imprint
Before my eyes
Instantly thunder cracked overhead
I flinched
And briefly wondered
If the heavens were rendered asunder
What would be revealed or released

Horned Moon

In pre-dawn darkness
a sickle of mellow light glides upwards
large as any newly risen full moon
taking my breath away

Horns cradle gold tissue
giving shape to her fullness

Saturn   Jupiter   Mercury
stand as sentinels
guardians to this mystical being
who draws prayers and homage
from all who are spellbound by the ethereal

Uncanny

I watch the unfolding mystery
Of a total eclipse of the moon

I puzzle over what is happening
I can't see – in my mind's eye –
How Sun   Moon   Earth all line up
Forgetting somehow
It is Earths shadow
Not Earth itself sliding across –
We haven't suddenly shifted from
Our usual orbit

It is an uncanny way
To measure the passing of time

Universe/Cosmos

We play with words
But it is no game
Definitions can change perception
Bring comfort or freedom

Universe felt so huge
There was no grasping of edges
Too many stars   galaxies
Too much space
Indifference between

Cosmos – not only a pretty flower
Another concept
An almost tangible presence
To send prayers of thanks to
A cry from the heart –
For courage and strength
A knowing we are not alone
Solitary beings – yes
But not alone
In the vastness of a universe

CPSIA information can be obtained
at www.ICGtesting.com
Printed in the USA
BVHW052312261222
655035BV00009B/272

9 781761 094606